# The Nearness of the Way You Look Tonight

# The Nearness of the Way You Look Tonight

## Charles North

Adventures in Poetry

Cover art by Joseph Cornell *Untitled* (*Coffeepot*),
courtesy of The University of Iowa Museum of Art

Distributed by
SPD: Small Press Distribution
1341 Seventh Street
Berkeley, CA 94710-1409
www.spdbooks.org

Revised edition, 2001
ADVENTURES IN POETRY
NEW YORK / BOSTON

www.adventuresinpoetry.com

ISBN 0-9706250-1-4

Some of these poems originally appeared in the following publications: *Barrow Street*, *Columbia*, *Columbia Poetry Review*, *Fourteen Hills: The SFSU Review*, *Hanging Loose*, *Lingo*, *Modern Painters*, *New American Writing*, *Sal Mimeo*, and *Shiny*.

The author is grateful to the Fund For Poetry for an award which helped support the writing of this book.

# CONTENTS

*for Mike*

THE PHILOSOPHY OF NEW JERSEY

*for Jill*

Actually the sky appears older than it is. It's 63 or 64 at most, not 75.
The part with the cliff face and the yellow crane could be in its
early 30s. It wasn't Wallace Stevens who said, "They have cut off my
head, and picked out all the letters of the alphabet — all the vowels
and consonants — and brought them out through my ears; and
then they want me to write poetry! I can't do it!" It was John Clare.
Wallace Stevens said — something like — the best poems are the
ones you meant to write. That has a nice sound to it, but it's hard to
see how he or anyone would know that. It would be hard, for ex-
ample, to accept the notion that there are ideas one meant to have.
Poems underneath every peeling sycamore and inside every file
cabinet, along with ideas about poetry and uncountable other ideas.

## THE NEARNESS OF THE WAY YOU LOOK TONIGHT

Smarter than morons are you
Shorter than giants

More reliable than bail-jumpers
Defter than those who are all thumbs

You are nicer than villains
Stabler than those with bipolar illness

Reedier than sousaphones or Eb horns
More fragrant than monkey houses

Saintlier than mass murderers are you
Peacefuller than janissaries

You are faster than tortoises
Tighter than muumuus

Newer than hand-me-downs
Cleaner than oil & grease stains

Hotter than meat lockers are you
More disinterested than investigative reporters

More heroic than cowards
Healthier than chronic patients

For you are prompter than no-shows
More alive than someone pushing up daisies

Freer than convicts are you
Stronger than weaklings

Svelter than nose tackles
More chivalrous than sentries

You are sprightlier than couch potatoes
More urban than dairy farmers

Rounder than flatworms
Apter than what is irrelevant

Finer than sackcloth are you
Gentler than torturers

Firmer than invertebrates
Kinglier than footmen

Fuller than vacuums are you
More staccato than slurred passages

You are more educable than dropouts
Roomier than crawlspaces

Humbler than showoffs
Closer than the big bang

Wittier than blockheads are you
More legal than after-hours bars

Barer than furnished apartments
Louder than quiet people

are you, more reliable than bail-jumpers,
pilloried for having one foot in the air

while the quidditists and eventualists
hole up looking a lot like the September mannerists,
although not as blossoming as the interventionists.

Speaking of bloom, the Chrysler Building equals
everything given away. And the windblown spandrels
unwind the air of pine angels.

CHAIN

Russia is the domed incantation of Kansas
As oceans burn in the individual day.

All day they came and went, sheep dog
Dogged social climber, sedulous

Luster after the Maison d'Infinite
In fine (it looks like) print, the curse of snowflakes.

Lakes abound in western and central Canada.
A part of it has the living tempo

Temporarily slowed, vibrant in
Ranting, the forte of carnations.

Nations become specific groves of ordinariness
Nestled between oceans of stupefaction

Action elbows, like the dark rainbow
Bowing in the new sky, clearing the inevitable

Table piled high with books and reels.
Real spring accumulates: not merely

Leaving the ground but including motion
Shunted previously to space...

To a space painted a smooth robin's egg blue.
Bluer than your eyes as you imagine them over the body

Described within this stirred world:
Whirled like letter-writing through a simpler day.

DAY AFTER DAY THE STORM MOUNTED. THEN IT DISMOUNTED

Suppose I am not the uplifter of all I uplift,
in the same sense that the coal-black sky, scumbled and showing a
    few red streaks,
doesn't exactly equal space.

The air is thick. Now it swirls.

It isn't air.

As in the *Iliad*,
death is continually swirling over
the bravest warriors from its source
in some tornado cellar or storage bin of death
and never in a straight line — as though it were embarrassed
to be seen for what it is and chose
the devious route. Not that
it can't directly target those whom it
chooses, but that it chooses not to.

A roughly trapezoidal shadow
has swirled up the side of the building opposite,
making its sooty brick facing darker than normally.
Some cars emerge from its insides.

One is making a left turn
from the extreme right lane.

When you think of the
truly instinctual moments, crying out
when the door slams on your foot,
or breathing deeply of spring, it seems only natural
to imagine an opposite way of behaving.

And when instinct is visible,
as clear in the air as leaves and water tanks,
it isn't inconceivable to suppose
an infinite number of possible worlds, bargained for, grasped,
and finally let go at the moment the situation
becomes clear, like storm clouds illuminating a herd of cows
nestled against coal-black tree trunks — *n'est-ce pas?*

And in composing for wind instruments
and putting the same or nearly the same chords
into two different pieces, you are
not likely to hear the same concert at noon
as at dusk — unless, of course, the performances are all illusion
and those in attendance merely marking time
within their own private band shells.

*Certo.*

An example of feeling
not quite taking the place of thought,
although memorized by it.

The house I live in.
The block of wood and the wood chips,
the surrounding proof that things exist outside the self
despite constant weeding. A waterfall of selves.

The mice are a nice touch, they don't have to speak in complete
    sentences.
Also the sawhorses.
One, sprinkled with life force,
took off a few minutes ago. Stung by its freedom,
whirling to gain a sense of direction,
it hovered over New Jersey for several seconds
before making a U turn.

No, you turn.

Does the name R. Penis Blavatsky mean anything, at all, to you?

Personally, I think
you need to focus on what is really important to you: change
habits as well as clothes. The shadows
that fall on wet rooftops altering them irrevocably,
new notions in hospital architecture,
half-built buildings with their shirt-sleeved inhabitants
in Italian movies of the sixties, etc.

You, with the neck that moved.
No, *you*; the shadows making their way

inside the paperweight, diffusing the glare that falls on
    upturned palm,
chin, cheek, even the occasional glancing blow
branching off into language.


Here you are a highly educated person. Hands, feet, chin,
    everything.


One morning, out of the blue,
a flock of wild turkeys
paraded up the hill from the road, at least forty
by actual count. The oddest thing was
their landing on the grass in small squads,
one at a time, with a parent figure
at either end, to march
steadily and without concern
for conceivably life-threatening surroundings
— in sharp contrast to the high-strung and
hyperactive deer — and just as suddenly
vanish into the mix of cedars and dark green shadows.


Here you resemble an aquamanile, your notions poached in
    rainwater.


Devoted dentist, darling chirurgeon, beloved branch manager,
dear critic, fragrant disciple,
esteemed concert mistress, caring strip miner,
wondrous instantiater, affectionate florist, moving engineer,

imaginative groundskeeper, tender restaurateur,
desirable glazier, charismatic coroner,
self-abnegating occultist, glowing restorer, lissome umpire…

Paper-thin traces of Being with needles sticking out of some but
   not all of them…

You, for example,
could be the Allegorical Figure of Taxation;
but more (I hope) about that later.

As Dizzy Gillespie is, or was, the god of the winds.

I am at a college interview. Each
of the interviewers is simultaneously
being interviewed. While she fields questions from all sides,
my interviewer shouts questions at me
from the far end of a long refectory table. I can
barely hear her over the din
but find myself admiring the way she responds to
those questions aimed directly at her. Then
I am face to face with someone who
asks if I prefer cloth- or paperbound books; but
just as I am about to respond he takes a wooden spoon
and flings some hard, uncooked grains of oatmeal towards the
   ceiling
where they hang suspended in the air
like a display of space matter in a planetarium.

Is that lighter — or just grayer?

In fact, for a long time
I've felt like apologizing
for what seem to me excessive references to darkness
as though the available light were on trial.
Sometimes it's virtually impossible
to get up in the morning. The days in
the middle of winter when it doesn't begin
to get light till 7 a.m. or even later,
the swirl commandeering hydrants, curbstones,
stoops, etc. To brush back shadows
from the cheek of night. "To be,"
as Thomas Browne wrote, "a kind of nothing
for a moment," a balloon with a beard....

Meanwhile, the cows on the postcard from the college bookstore
have moved from in front of a clump
of shade trees to somewhere more virtual. Peasants
looking stoned, lying face up underneath a table groaning with
    food,
searching the invisible sky as well as each other
for clues regarding their current state: one of
pleasant stupor, or stupefied fullness,
as symbolized in the dazed-looking
small game and surreal life forms attending the postmortem
of what has clearly been a positive experience
for most of them — although not without a trace of some

prior violence, most obviously in long broken cudgels
but also in a branch bent like a catapult
and in the dizzying angle, everything
about to topple into the whirlpool or quicksand of satisfaction
inside which a pipe can tip over a table. (*Das Schlaraffenland*,
    1567)

Not exactly pleasant
but not entirely unpleasant either.
Somewhat like "turning over
in your grave." The breeze tingling.

I don't think the subject has changed significantly.

I'm thinking of a noun,
any noun. I picture it
as hard rubber, darkly resinous,
the same family, roughly speaking, as Being-in-Itself.

Each of the slots can be and is filled
by a person, place, thing
or other suitable substantive.

Currently the slots come with appropriate hat sizes,
5 1/2 being one of the most popular (Beauty in itself
being rather stupid, in case you haven't already noticed).

While you were painting
the rather severe downpour stopped.

Slowed first, to avoid jolting
the already battered air conditioners.
I don't know about you
but I frequently have the feeling
that the buildings are mere skin, bruised by dusk,
little by little powerless to do
more than ripple, comparable to the rippling that erupts out of
    flatness
to be rolled out and attenuated like the most attenuated
of clouds. What moments are to
themselves: not so much moving as scaffolding.

How do you *know*
or can you *prove*
that the evening doesn't subsist on pure will —
short and fat, thick-necked,
wheezing like a woodchuck, its inner
life a barrel vault, clinging to the last chord played,
the last note written?

In Smokey Joe's Café.

To put it in epic terms — Thinkology
but once removed. How anyone comes to live in
a world of oxbows, steppes, wheat fields, and projective versts.

For you are the electronic type: your keys are oxblood and
    celadon stars.

I see, or am beginning to,

that your reliance on night is genuflectory.

But so do the dark references

resemble life: life after death.

How

it is possible

and also impossible to be the imagination

of a future time. Which is to say that,

given a little more time,

the consequences for both city and rural life

can and must distinguish themselves — unlike the beauties of New
    Hampshire

arm in arm with the beauties of Vermont.

A ball of frosted light

just whirled over the Hudson,

coming to rest on a lamp post. Which

bats it to another. The maroon

of a coffee shop awning utterly divorced from

its lower extenders, barely visible, like the bouffant of an
    angel

or as Dorothy Wordsworth reported

of an especially beautiful May afternoon, "I drank

a little Brandy and water, and was in heaven."

Clearly not the same as

landing in the middle of Herald Square

wearing Valkyrie gear and dancing a pavanne
to celebrate the sudden change in seasons.

Still,
comparison to the other arts seems
all but inevitable, as witness the so-called
Clarinetist's Fallacy, coaxing excessive
feeling out of what is essentially a cold instrument
if brilliantly so — the result being a whining
masquerading as feeling

whereas the best playing is "cold and passionate
as the dawn."

"The reed is held on the mouthpiece
by a soft rubber support which has sluts.
A very pure dound is obtained by an metallic plate
mounled directly behind of the rubber support.
The whole device is in the form of a flexible band very
    resistant
adjusted by two screws, to allow adjustment for personal
    playing styles...

> — casy sound production
> — a very rich sounding note
> — a naturally obstained pure sound.

A/Remove the adjusting screurs
B/Place the reed on the mathpiece
C/Carefully position the ligature around the mountpiece
　　　plus reed
D/Fit the crews and tighten..." [sic]


Foghorns in the atmosphere
of Smokey Joe's Café. In
or just behind it, in an alleyway
lined with stucco and graffiti from the sixties.


As the life force plays tricks
plus the two Brahms Sonatas for clarinet (or viola) and piano.


Some whiteness is beginning
to show around the edges
but not in all places at once.
The bills have been paid; Mozart
is playing quietly in the background
aged 2 1/2; a few of the dark clumps, wads of emptiness,
anchor the deer and the echoing cedars. A few
more particles than usual: to put aside, focus on, or just
chuck out never and nowhere to be witnessed again ever.


Your lids are getting heavy.
People carrying water faucets keep attempting to put you out.


North of the Charles...

My name,
actually my middle name, is Alphonse
and I live in northern Alberta,
but have a summer palace near Albuquerque.
Of adobe. Behind the brickwork.

The close colors depart in droves.

To write
                    a nation or thriving city-state.
The Queen Anne's Lace
                            dove in.

Meanwhile, deer consumption
— by and not of —
has proceeded at a fairly alarming rate.
Nearing the surface they chin upwards
slicing the air into deer and not-deer. Pruning
to within an inch of life, which in this case
happens to read as broad daylight
despite a charcoal gray fuzz directly overhead
like a sweater on a minaret.

You have received a grant to do hornet work...
standing on your head
not to mention endless attention to the shivers
that erupt. There was a just stained look to the sky
that lasted most of the morning, leaving
rags at the edges. Not merely cloud shreds

or broccoli-covered cliffs; the perforations
through which the breeze enters like woodwinds: the bright
    glow of new leaves
magnetizing unspeakably charged states of being.

Just before dusk,
a whole notebookful of sense impressions flitted around
the trunk of a maple tree,
a fairly young one,
looking for a hole in the protective wrapping.

A woman in a cream-colored blouse and blue apron
bends at a 90° angle to fill a lustrous pitcher from a copper-
    colored urn.
Leaning out the window the evening clouds floated by.

Devoted dentist, darling chirurgeon, beloved mailman,
dear critic, fragrant disciple,
esteemed second violinist, caring strip miner,
delightful bagman, wondrous instantiater,
affectionate florist, moving engineer, embraceable barber,
imaginative umpire, tender restaurateur,
desirable glazier, lissome dwarf, humble go-getter,
self-abnegating groundskeeper, glowing restorer, tender agent,
ravishing dunner, adored kayaker,
considerate bathing beauty, warm slam-dunker, delicate rabbi,
undisgruntled grant applier, tasteful chastiser,
huggable frontier scout, kind futurist, lively thief,
haunting numismatist, glistening bartender,
full-breasted chairperson, melting dealer, translucent branch
    manager,
angelic burgomaster, generous do-it-yourselfer,
herniating operatic tenor, congenial wide receiver,
exemplary bailiff, stimulating mobster, cute rum-runner,
willowy executionist, life-promoting tour guide,
handy antagonist, caressed misprizer,
cherished innkeeper, head-turning pharmacist,
ached-for sous chef, unforgettable fogie, seductive pointillist,
riveting sophist, missed beadle, magnetic muezzin,
well-meaning bowler, dedicated phrenologist,
precious typist, seraphic song stylist, winsome CEO,
idolized quick study, dearly beloved test pilot,
undetested laundress, pet decoder, lovesome party leader

33

PHILOSOPHICAL SONGS

1. Some of Them That Do Fish Will Go for a Midnight Swim

It's not so much the partis pris as
the performance which is then called into question.
Then back to the dents. Embrace of atmosphere

which isn't the wind that collects on the windowpane,
the word skidding dispassionately by way of
your gown of powder blue light. The cedars slip.


2. As Moonlight Becomes You

refining the swale for the sake of
ordinary life, which isn't orderly
but does undergo a pattern of resolute change
because you supply the necessity: hence

ordinary life which isn't orderly,
marches on ahead into a swirl of reddening leaves
because you supply the necessity. Hence
the moon is rampant, flitting between you.

### 3. Madrigal

Not border or pass — not quite
       past either, post? postern? as
in the past reaching around its
turquoise plinth despite a coating of melted pine needles
or are they melting meanwhile the landscape has turned
       arrow-like to waste.

Distant squawks and pained foothills
not painted, not *intricately*
personal at best. Yet a morsel
off the top of a silo, flung from a train
closer than phenomenology more rapid than song.

The things you had no right to do, the things you should have
    done,
Of cities leaping to stature, of fame like a flag unfurled
And a city all a-smoulder and…as if it really mattered.
And the greasy smoke in an inky cloak went streaking down the
    sky.

It sort of made me think a bit, that story that you told
All glamour, grace and witchery, all passion verve and glow,
The all-but-fluid silence, — yet the longing grows and grows.
Now wouldn't you expect to find a man an awful crank!

For the debit side's increasing in a most alarming way
From the vastitudes where the world protrudes through clouds like
    seas up-shoaled.
So the stranger stumbles across the room, and flops down there
    like a fool
Dreaming alone of a people, dreaming alone of a day.

The Wanderlust has haled me from the morris chairs of ease
By the darkness that just drowns you, by the wail of home desire.
It's also true I longed for you and wrote it on an egg…
Though where I don't exactly know, and don't precisely care.

It seems it's been since the beginning; it seems it will be to
  the end
To hit the high spots sometimes, and to let your chances slip.
For the lake is yonder dreaming, and my cabin's on the shore.
In the little Crimson Manual it's written plain and clear:

We're merely "Undesirables," artistic more or less,
The people ever children, and the heavens ever blue,
Dear ladies, if I saw you now I'd turn away my face
Oh, the clammy brow of anguish! the livid, foam-flecked lips!

I'm not so wise as the lawyer guys, but strictly between us two
I'm the Steinway of strange mischief. We're all brutes more or
  less.
Then you've a hunch what the music meant…hunger and night and
  the stars.
All honey-combed, the river ice was rotting down below.

LINES

Technically unwinding its purchase power
despite the roofs and their allover blind,
pronouncing an effect of vines

bearing grapes at intervals backwards
to the mostly distressed values,
private interest coterminous with public leaching out

to enlist the mobile freedoms,
of increased expectancy including but not confined
to putting the numbers in line,

while the slick streets are being swept
by all the emotional legwork to be done,
who and what final wrangling with the gap

between sure deadline and unsecured future
captioned in irises, while the qualifiers
push on ahead, any organ defined or implied by work

that hits home at the first pragmatics,
threatening a wheat field or sudden burst of spring
dripping color along a riveted earth.

## Note on Fog

I like Augustine's calling lust a "fog." Of course he didn't say it in English and didn't call it embarrassing. I also like the image of the critic who wouldn't know a poem if it came up and bit him. I picture him, or her, not necessarily an evil person, having finished some minor chore like taking out the garbage, when this *thing* strikes. The fog of surprise and not, at least relatively speaking, the blood or teeth marks. The utter disorientation, seeing things and not seeing anything.

wearing a robe, and then getting rid of it. The French *enrobé*, meaning so thick it has to be licked off. Last night was robed in a thick, grainy fog that dissipated late this morning. Even so, the air isn't quite itself, shielded from its deepest concerns — and from a few superficial ones as well. In my judgement, or judge-a-ment as former President Gerald Ford used to pronounce it, echoing the traditional tripartite division of mental faculties, it's going to clear up, but probably not before the middle of the afternoon. Also in the judge-a-ment of the local TV forecaster. What moral philosophers since Plato have deemed judge-a-ment as powerful as will ("the strongest oaths" being "straw to the fire i´ the blood"), i.e., serious rivals for moral attention? Sometimes what appears to be judge-a-ment is robed in sleep, or something resembling it. A grainy fog casting everything in a gray blur. Then someone named Moriarty steps out of the grain, his thought processes enrobed in mystery, shedding fog in spangles of black-and-white.

## A STANZA FOR BRODEY

The canvas of impossible feelings wrapped in bacon fat
whose laminates sprawl smack into the muck,
and your silkier villains are the disconsolates,
sweating out the most recent Styx,
blindsided by oak trees and the triumphal ridge
like the tryst between anti-matter and hawks in sunshine.

ATTRIBUTES OF POETRY

*for Marjorie Welish*

1

The Floridas of the soul

Not the mental Floridas the Floridas that happen to brush by on
the street wearing musk and little else

2

For the sun goes down its hairline studded with cumquats

3

One of several fissures like reading aloud to a horse

What of the head the head is lost in thought

4

What of the feet navigating through quicksand not necessarily of
their own choosing

What of the little world of the eye

5

Circumscribed

That people had brains at least until quite recently

6

Use pectin in a sentence
They were pectin like sardines
The robins pectin the trees all day and all night


7

He pectin a terrible hurry


8

Nicer than villains taller than inchworms faster than slowpokes
More opaque than Philip Johnson's Glass House


9

Striding towards Eleusinian life have you noticed how much *detail*
    goes into paralleling the flow of earth
The last two summers were in fact quite nice


10

If not an angel in a business suit then diopters of space and
    time
Attractive deer with on-site experience seeks new orientation the
    darker and more galluptious the better


11

The slipcase for a few minor league stars

12

Taking courses

Where one course ends and another course begins

What it means to be a course (what it would be *like* to be a
course)


13

History minus the stopping equaling a kind of prehistory

Or medium in which it is possible to frame units of pre-judgement


14

A kind of solid space with feathers sticking out

TRIO FROM WANG WEI

*for Larry Fagin*


1. Mullion Hotel

The roof raises its music stand at ease.
Dormers unscrolling their window boxes.
Kick the confusion along the ramp, through the antennae!
To presage you while your plié breaks out in morning glories.


2. Lightness Eye

The gong shampoos the January rain.
Then, when you are rendered like song,
Fence-sitting (lying —) like Russian linen,
Foo! Show the king the tea of shame!


3. Character As Character

The hills are bare you can't make out anyone,
Still as sounds form persons the air is all conversation,
The forest of sunset licks its way inward.
Above the north-facing moss the sky is green, black — and blue! —
   ribbon.

INITIAL N

Artifice,
Fistulous

Luster,
Tergiversation

Shunning machinery
Re storms and

Sand-like oriels.
All reels

(*Ils attendent*)
A tendency

Seeded with
Withholdings.

Inks deafened
Indoors

Or seized evidence:
A dense star

Starring Diderots,
Roses to summon

Monsters,
Ersatz eyes.

I sing the gingkoes
Cozy (human — ) as

Asterisks,
Risks inside art.

LANDSCAPE & CHARDIN

*for Trevor Winkfield*

I have to confess that *Bon appétit* never strikes me as an appropri-
ate invitation. It seems too…medicinal, like charging a poem
with the obligation to improve, or at least define, one's sense of
self. Speaking of which, how many of our great poets are them-
selves more than 8% of the time? Not just the obvious cases. Take
Yeats. Or take Hart Crane. Take almost anyone. I don't feel as
confident saying so, but I'm pretty sure the same is true for paint-
ers even if the percentages go up some. So much of what we
experience as present is earmarked for the future. Sing, Contin-
gency, of a single membrane in the process of becoming a frame
house open to the charcoal and cantaloupe of evening — of the
unfavored nation status of line. I like the idea that the air is too
close to either prove or disprove its existence, and that it has no
stake whatever in the issue. The deer are practically pets. A few
days ago, the small one that lay down to die got up when no one
was looking. No one ever sees a live skunk, yet we take the facts
of its life on the evidence. Along with a certain amount of shiv-
ering and pure, or at least uncharacterizable, *qualia*. The impres-
sions planted before the realms collide. Still, the houses, linear or
not, retain a humanity despite their continuity with anything
and everything, power and phone lines as much as faraway loose-
strife whose color (whatever else it may take cover under) floods
the eye. The pond calmed down earlier. Written on in only a few
spots apart from the questionable egrets — living question marks
is what I mean. I don't, personally, see much suffering other than

the everpresent kind. I can envision the Incredible Shrinking Man, by now not so incredible, up to his neck in ground cover or the dried up stalks showing above the pond surface, barely taking in the postings against deer-hunting, the freeze-frames of the hawks, the occasional ghostly flock of wild turkeys among the ubiquitous cedars — plus hints of yet-to-be-instantiated structure. The lintels, what there is of them, are heartbreaking.

including the pond bitten down to its cuticles,
whatever you were doing pursuant to flatness

it doesn't mean we exist as writing.
What is flat is on trial for its flatness.
Whatever you were doing pursuant to flatness

is a particular: it is its own witness.
While air billows and closes around the petal of evening

(whatever you were doing pursuant to flatness)
it doesn't mean we exist as writing
— fringed in charcoal and umber fields, loosestrife utterly
    mismanaged.

Book design & composition by
t y p e s l o w l y
Printed by McNaughton & Gunn.
Typeset in Bembo. Printed in an edi-
tion of 500 copies. A special edition
is lettered A-Z, in boards, and signed
by the author.